VIJAYSHREE R

When Children Forget, Life Remembers

A journey of healing for parents left behind

All illustrations in this book were generated with the assistance of AI tools. The characters appearing in these images are symbolic and illustrative, not exact portrayals of real people. While Jagdish and Lalitha are inspired by the author's parents, the visuals are not intended to represent their precise appearance, age, or identity.

This story, and the experiences it shares, is meant for all parents who have lovingly raised their children and now face the quietness of being left behind. The images are used purely as creative aids to support the storytelling. The reflections, lessons, and wisdom in this book are real and drawn from the timeless teachings of the Bhagavad Gita.

First edition

ISBN: 978-93-344-1770-8

This book was professionally typeset on Reedsy.
Find out more at reedsy.com

To my beloved parents and my Kaka(Uncle) –
who lived for their children,
loved quietly, gave selflessly,
and now wait with eyes full of grace,
surrounded by memories.
This is for the quiet hearts
that beat unheard in old rooms,
for the hands that once held everything
and are now empty.
This is not just a story –
it is my prayer for your healing.
May it be a mirror,
a balm,
a way back to love.

– Vijayshree

"The Bhagavad Gita offers guidance for every stage of life, helping us navigate challenges with grace, wisdom, and love. Through the journey of Jagdish and Lalitha, all parents who have given selflessly and now find themselves waiting are invited to awaken to their own purpose, reclaim their inner strength, and rediscover fulfillment beyond roles and expectations. May this timeless wisdom illuminate your path, bringing peace, love, and harmony to your heart and home."

-Vijayshree Ratanparkhe

Contents

Foreword

For All Silent Pillars of Love

There is a certain kind of love in this world that asks for nothing in return — the kind we receive quietly from our parents. It doesn't arrive with grand declarations. It shows up in everyday sacrifices, half-eaten meals, sleepless nights, and prayers whispered in silence. This love forms the invisible spine of our lives — the reason we could stand tall, even when we forgot who held us up.

But in today's fast-moving world, these pillars are often left behind at deserted stations. Once the providers of dreams and security, they now sit alone — waiting for a phone call, a visit, or even a simple acknowledgment. This book is not just a story. It is a reminder. A reflection. A mirror held up to us all.

We may not be able to undo what's been done. But we can *pause*. We can *remember*. And we can return — not just physically, but emotionally and spiritually — to those who once stood as our roots.

This work is dedicated to **every parent** who gave their all, and is still waiting — without complaint, without blame, with only love in their eyes.

May this book become a gentle call — not of guilt, but of awakening.

With folded hands,
Vijayshree

Preface

The Journey of Jagdish & Lalitha: A Story of Forgotten Stations and Eternal Love

When I began writing this story, it was not born from imagination. It arose from a deeper, divine experience — shaped by the quiet realities of countless parents I have seen, and the silent sacrifices that often go unnoticed in our world. Jagdish and Lalitha are not just characters. They are representations of every mother and father who sacrificed dreams so their children could fly, yet now sit in silence as those very children forget the way back home.

This book is not meant to accuse or blame. It is meant to *heal.* To *awaken.* To bridge the gap between generations, between expectations and reality, between karma and emotion.

Through the metaphor of a train journey, each chapter unveils layers of human experience — from attachment to detachment, ego to empathy, sorrow to spiritual insight. At its heart lies the eternal wisdom of the Bhagavad Gita — not as a scripture to preach, but as a map for everyday life and emotional navigation.

This story was written with one prayer:

That every reader may find a part of themselves in these pages — whether as the child, the parent, or the one in between.

If this book stirs a memory, rekindles a phone call, or evokes a tear — then perhaps, it has done its work.

With deep reverence to all the elders who still wait without bitterness,

And to the divine who witnesses it all in quiet grace.

— Vijayshree(Founder of Shree's Essencia)

Prologue

The courtyard was hushed. The old swing hung still beneath the mango tree, and neem leaves floated slowly to the ground. Jagdish and Lalitha sat side by side on the veranda, tea growing cold in their hands, hearts heavy with quiet longing. Their son, Arjun, had moved far away—first for studies, then work, then a life of his own. The love, care, and sacrifices of years seemed to have faded into the background of his busy world.

And yet… a soft, quiet voice stirred within them: *"There is more to this journey than waiting."*

Life, they began to understand, is not a single destination. It is a moving train, and every day, every feeling, every memory is a compartment waiting to be explored.

This is the story of Jagdish and Lalitha. A story of love, of letting go, of discovering purpose beyond expectations. A story that shows us that when children forget, life remembers—and sometimes, the journey back to ourselves is the most important one of all.

Introduction

Jagdish and Lalitha are not just characters; they are symbolic mirrors for every parent who has given everything and now sits quietly, wondering if it mattered. Through their eyes, we witness the pain of neglect, the temptation to compare, and the journey from attachment to self-discovery.

Guided by the eternal wisdom of the Bhagavad Gita, this book is a gentle companion — not to blame, but to awaken. Each chapter is a "station" of reflection:

- *The Boarding Platform* — recognizing loss and purpose
- *The Reserved Seat* — reclaiming Swadharma and self-worth
- Further stations explore detachment, inner peace, and closure

Though the story uses the metaphor of a train journey, it is not about traveling physically; it is about **moving inward, reflecting, and reconnecting with one's own life and dharma**.

This journey invites you, the reader, to step off the platform of waiting and onto the path of remembering — your value, your purpose, your peace.

One

The Boarding Platform – The Forgotten Purpose

Based on the Principle of Purushartha: Dharma, Artha, Kama, Moksha

"The Empty Swing in the Courtyard" – Jagdish & Lalitha's Journey Begins

The Echo of Silence – Waiting in the Courtyard

The once lively courtyard of Jagdish and Lalitha's ancestral home now echoed with silence. The old swing that used to sway with the laughter of their son, Arjun, stood still under the mango tree. The neem shed its leaves slowly onto the earth like forgotten letters. Birds still chirped, the sun still rose, but for the couple, the days merged into a slow, silent wait.

Arjun had moved to the US years ago. First for studies. Then for work. Then marriage. Phone calls became shorter, festivals turned into forwarded WhatsApp messages, and visits became "next year for sure, Baba."

One afternoon, Lalitha broke down.

"He's forgotten us," she whispered, wiping her tears with the end of her cotton saree.

Jagdish, a retired Sanskrit teacher known for his quiet strength, sat motionless. "We did everything for him, didn't we? Saved every rupee, sacrificed every dream, gave him the best education. And now? We are not even part of his priorities."

The Visitor – Wisdom Knocks

That evening, as they sat on their veranda sipping tea in silence, an old friend stopped by — Shastriji, the priest from the nearby temple. He had seen their dimmed faces too many times and decided to stop by.

He looked at the dusty tulsi plant in the corner, the untouched

Bhagavad Gita on the table, and then gently settled onto the floor beside them.

"I see this often now," he said softly. "Parents left behind. Children chasing dreams. But the Gita reminds us — life is not one goal, but four: the *Purusharthas*."

Jagdish nodded slowly, "Dharma, Artha, Kama, Moksha… I taught those Purusharthas for years."

"Yes," Shastriji said, "but many mistake the journey for the destination. Arjun is caught in *Artha* (material pursuit) and *Kama* (desires), forgetting *Dharma* (duty) and the higher purpose of *Moksha* (liberation)."

Lalitha's Question – "What about us?"

Lalitha looked up, her eyes brimming with hurt and hope.

"So what do we do now, Shastriji? Just wait for a call? Accept this as karma?"

Shastriji shook his head gently, his eyes full of compassion.

"No, Lalitha beti. This is your platform too — not just Arjun's. Remember, Purushartha is not just for the young chasing dreams. It's for everyone. Even now, your life has purpose. You are not abandoned. You are being redirected."

He paused and added, "This is your Dharma now — not to cling, but to contribute. Not to wait, but to walk forward on your own path. Even at this stage of life, you are boarding a new train — one toward deeper peace, selfless service, and spiritual preparation."

The Inner Train – Realization Begins

That night, Jagdish stood silently near the old swing in their courtyard, lost in thought. Lalitha walked out slowly, holding two steel glasses of tea.

They sat in silence, like every evening. But tonight was heavier — yet somehow also lighter.

Arjun had messaged a hurried, "Sorry, work call again," when they tried to video chat. Another festival had passed. Another year without his visit.

"Did we do something wrong?" Lalitha asked softly.

"No," Jagdish replied, "We gave him everything."

Suddenly, Shastriji's words echoed in his heart:

"Life is like a train. The Gita says we board it with four goals — Dharma, Artha, Kama, Moksha. Most people get stuck at Artha and Kama… and forget to continue toward Dharma and Moksha."

Jagdish imagined Arjun on a fast train in America — collecting wealth, building a family, chasing success — but missing the essence of life's deeper journey. Not out of selfishness, but forgetfulness.

The New Platform – Reclaiming Dharma

That same night, Jagdish dusted off his old teaching notes. He had once taught dozens of children Sanskrit verses and Gita slokas. Students still remembered him.

Lalitha opened her notebook of recipes and bhajans. She remembered the widows' ashram nearby and wondered if she could teach them simple songs, or just sit and listen.

Suddenly, they weren't just waiting.

They were preparing.

Not for Arjun's return — but for their own journey forward.

The Forgotten Purpose – Embracing Moksha

They began to realize:

- **Artha** (Wealth) is useful, but temporary.
- **Kama** (Pleasure) brings joy, but fades.
- **Dharma** (Righteous duty) gives meaning and direction.
- **Moksha** (Inner freedom) is not a destination — it is the quiet peace within.

They had not been left behind by life.

They had been invited into the next station of it.

They had been shown their own train.

Reflection & Realization for Parents:

Problem Experienced:

Emotional neglect and feelings of abandonment by children settled abroad.

Gita Insight:

The four *Purusharthas* (Dharma, Artha, Kama, Moksha) are not just for youth. Life becomes painful when Artha and Kama are pursued without Dharma or awareness of Moksha.

Lesson for Parents:

Your life is not over because your children moved on. Reconnect to your *own* Dharma. This phase is an invitation to deepen your spiritual path, contribute to society, and rediscover self-worth beyond roles.

Practical Steps:

- Start reading the Gita or spiritual texts regularly
- Begin service in your community — like helping an orphanage or temple
- Teach something you know: music, cooking, wisdom, culture
- Journal, reflect, or start satsangs with others in similar situations

Closing Thought:

"When your children forget your worth, it's time to remember your own."

The train of Purushartha never stops — but it waits for you to remember your seat.

Two

The Reserved Seat – Remembering Your Swadharma

Based on the Principle of Swadharma: One's Unique Duty

"The Reserved Compartment of the Soul" – Jagdish & Lalitha's Next Realization

The Misplaced Ticket – The Temptation to Compare

The next morning, Jagdish sat on the veranda bench, his hands holding an old album of photos. Lalitha brought tea again, but this time, she was irritated. "Did you see Meena's daughter from our lane? She's visiting from Canada — took her parents on a temple trip, shared photos online. People commented 'such sanskaari kids.' Look at us!"

Jagdish didn't respond. He closed the album and looked at the neem leaves swaying overhead.

Lalitha's voice cracked, "Why don't we get that kind of love? Did we raise him wrong?"

Silence hung heavy until Jagdish replied, "Maybe… we're sitting in the wrong seat, Lalitha."

"What?"

He gently said, "Swadharma. Our unique path. Maybe we're expecting Arjun to fulfill duties that were never his seat to begin with."

The Conductor's Lesson – Shastriji Returns

Later that day, Shastriji returned with a tiffin of prasad. Seeing their tired faces, he sat down again. "I came to share a verse," he said, "Gita 3.35 — '*Better to do one's own duty imperfectly than another's perfectly.*' That is Swadharma."

Lalitha frowned, "But isn't it Arjun's Swadharma to take care of us?"

Shastriji smiled. "Yes — *when he remembers it.* But your Swadharma as parents was to nurture. You did that beautifully. Now, holding on and trying to direct his path is no longer your Dharma — it's a borrowed duty."

Jagdish looked up, "So we've been sitting in someone else's compartment?"

"Exactly," said Shastriji. "Each soul boards this life with a reserved seat — a unique role based on their nature. When we try to sit in another's seat — by controlling their path, judging their choices — discomfort comes. Acceptance of one's own Dharma brings peace."

Lalitha's Pain - "So we just let go?"

"But how do we stop caring?" Lalitha whispered. "Isn't it our job to worry for our son?"

"No," Shastriji said gently. "It was your role to guide, not to control. You are not surrendering love — you are surrendering attachment to how it 'should' look. That's the difference between bondage and freedom. Love without control is Swadharma in action."

Jagdish's Flashback - A Seat of His Own

That night, Jagdish opened his journal. He remembered the young version of himself — standing in a small classroom, chalk in hand, explaining Sanskrit slokas with passion. Back then, he felt alive. Aligned. Not waiting for appreciation — just doing his Swadharma.

He turned to Lalitha and said, "I was happy when I taught. Not because students praised me, but because I was in my seat."

She smiled, "Then maybe… it's time I find my own seat again too."

The Shift - Reclaiming Their Own Dharma

The next few days, the couple began making small changes.

Jagdish visited the nearby school and offered to teach slokas once a week. The children laughed, mispronounced verses, and asked innocent questions that warmed his heart.

Lalitha joined a local temple women's group — leading bhajans, sharing recipes, laughing after months of numb silence.

Each day felt lighter. Not because Arjun called — but because they weren't waiting anymore. They were finally seated in their own train compartment — their **Swadharma**.

The Soul's Reserved Seat – A Deeper Freedom

They learned to stop comparing their journey with others. The world had different kinds of children, different expressions of love.

What mattered was this: **Their seat was never empty. They had simply forgotten to sit in it.**

Reflection & Realization for Parents:

Problem Experienced:

Comparison, resentment, and loss of self-worth when children do not behave as expected — especially when other parents seem better cared for.

Gita Insight (3.35):

"It is better to fail in one's own duty than to succeed in another's."

Swadharma is about embracing one's unique path and letting go of imposed roles or expectations.

Lesson for Parents:

You were born with a purpose beyond parenting. Once that karma is complete, your next dharma begins. Don't sit in someone else's seat — reclaim your own identity, gifts, and purpose.

Practical Steps:

- Ask: "What made me feel purposeful before?" Revisit that.
- Stop comparing your child to others — their karma is not yours.
- Write a list of your strengths and see how they can serve others.
- Volunteer, teach, sing, lead — occupy your seat.

Closing Thought:

"Peace doesn't come from your child fulfilling their duty — it comes from you remembering yours."

In the Train of Life, no one else can sit in your Reserved Seat. Claim it — before the journey ends.

Three

The Coach Identity – Rediscovering Who You Really Are

Jagdish Rao,
Retired
Sanskrit Lecturer

Based on the Principle of Varna & Gunas: Beyond Roles, Into Essence

"The Nametag Nobody Saw" – Jagdish & Lalitha's Third Realization

The Vanishing Nameplate – When Roles Fade

One Sunday afternoon, Jagdish stood near the entrance of their house, polishing the rusting nameplate:

"Jagdish Rao, Retired Sanskrit Lecturer"

The letters were fading. Just like his identity.

Lalitha stepped out with a cup of tea. "That nameplate won't shine like before," she said.

Jagdish nodded, eyes distant. "Sometimes I wonder… who am I now? Just 'Arjun's father'? A forgotten teacher?"

That evening, a neighbor's child visited and addressed him casually, "Uncle, is Arjun coming for Diwali this year?"

Before Jagdish could answer, the boy had already run off to play.

He looked down at his feet. Something inside ached — not just from age, but from invisibility.

The Train of Roles – Shastriji's Analogy

The next day, Jagdish and Lalitha found themselves sitting with Shastriji again under the neem tree. Jagdish shared his thoughts.

"I feel… blank. No one needs my lectures. No students. No office. Arjun rarely calls. Who am I now, really?"

Shastriji smiled gently, "Jagdish ji, have you ever been inside a train's coach where people forget their destination because they get too absorbed in the seat number, the AC switch, the view?"

He continued, "All of us are in a train of life — and each coach represents a role: father, husband, teacher, friend. But none of these are the train itself. The coach is where you serve, not who you are."

Lalitha asked, "Then what are we?"

"Souls," Shastriji said softly. "Passengers on a divine journey. The roles are just compartments. You are not the coach — you are the traveler."

Lalitha's Worry – "So We Just Stop Being Parents?"

"But we spent everything to raise him," Lalitha said, her voice trembling. "It feels like we were only meant to be parents… and now that's gone."

Shastriji looked at her kindly. "Parenthood was your Varna-expression — your nature expressing itself through nurturing and protecting. But the soul has more to express. The Bhagavad Gita teaches that each soul carries three gunas — sattva, rajas, tamas — and a nature that unfolds in seasons."

He paused, then added, "When one role ends, another begins. You are still creators, still givers, still guides — maybe not for Arjun, but for someone else who needs light."

Jagdish's Moment – The Forgotten Chalkboard

That night, Jagdish walked past the old storeroom and found his teaching slate and chalk — kept from his school days. He held them, as if holding a part of his own soul.

Suddenly, he remembered how alive he used to feel writing shlokas on a dusty blackboard, explaining metaphors from the Gita to sleepy teenagers. Not for salary. Not for status. But for the joy of it.

"I was more than a father," he whispered. "I was a teacher. I was a transmitter of light."

Reclaiming Inner Identity – New Passengers

Over the next week, Jagdish began tutoring two neighborhood kids in Sanskrit — not for money, but because he wanted to.

Lalitha visited the widow's home again, not as someone "left behind," but as someone ready to sing, share, and simply listen.

They were no longer just "Arjun's parents." They were **Jagdish and Lalitha** — souls with gifts, wisdom, presence, and purpose.

The Nametag Within – A New Light

Lalitha stood before the mirror one morning, tying her saree with care.

"Who are you dressing up for?" Jagdish teased.

"For the bhajan group," she smiled. "They asked me to lead today."

He smiled back. "Lead well. They don't know yet — but they're in the presence of a queen."

They laughed. But in that moment, a silent truth was felt:

The roles may have shifted…

…but their **real identity** had finally reawakened.

Reflection & Realization for Parents:

Problem Experienced:

Loss of identity after retirement or after children grow distant — leading to depression or confusion about self-worth.

Gita Insight (Varna & Gunas):

Your role is not your self. You are a soul beyond labels. Varna is based not on birth, but on inner qualities — thinking, building, protecting, serving. These keep evolving with age and karma.

Lesson for Parents:

You are more than "just a parent." Don't confuse the seat you sit in with the soul you are. Your purpose continues. Your energy, love, wisdom — they're needed elsewhere too.

Practical Steps:

- Reflect: "What identity have I clung to that no longer serves me?"
- List: "What did I love doing before roles consumed me?"
- Reclaim: Serve where your inner nature (guna) feels alive — teaching, mentoring, nurturing.
- Affirm daily: "I am not my role. I am a soul — a traveler with gifts to offer."

Closing Thought:

"When the world forgets your name tag — it's the perfect time to remember your soul tag."

You're not the train. Not the seat. You're the traveler — divine, eternal, evolving.

Four

The Journey Segments – Knowing Life's True Stations

Brahmacharya Grihastha Vanaprastha Sannyasa

Based on the Principle of Ashrama: Brahmacharya, Grihastha, Vanaprastha, Sannyasa

"The Forest in the Heart" – Jagdish & Lalitha Step into Vanaprastha

The Silent Clock – Time That No One Notices

Jagdish looked at the old pendulum clock on the wall. It had stopped ticking a week ago, but neither he nor Lalitha had noticed. Days had begun to blur. Meals happened out of habit, evenings melted into quiet, and celebrations were memories more than events.

Lalitha sat across the room, gently folding a saree. Her hands paused.

"We used to rush so much during Arjun's school days, remember?" she said.

Jagdish smiled faintly. "I remember ironing his shirt every morning at 6:30 sharp. He used to grumble about the chilly bathroom tiles."

The smile faded.

"Now," he said, "I sometimes feel like we're waiting for something… but I don't know what."

Shastriji's Visit – A Map of the Four Stages

Later that evening, Shastriji visited again. This time he carried a small copper bowl of tulsi water and a few jaggery sweets.

"I thought today we talk not about children, but about *you*," he said, settling down on the floor.

"You've crossed Brahmacharya – the student stage. You lived the Grihastha life — householder, parents, workers. But now…" he paused, "You are in *Vanaprastha*. The third stage. The forest dweller — not physically, but mentally."

Lalitha looked confused. "Forest? But we are still in this house. Still cooking, cleaning, waiting."

"Exactly," said Shastriji. "Vanaprastha doesn't mean you move to a jungle. It means you slowly withdraw from *expecting* from the world — especially from family. You begin walking toward God."

Jagdish's Resistance – "So we're no longer needed?"

Jagdish stirred. "So we become irrelevant? Is that what scripture says?"

Shastriji's voice remained soft. "Not irrelevant, Jagdish. Just... redirected. You're not meant to *chase* your children anymore. You're meant to *guide* yourself. The Gita shows four stations in life. If we cling to the earlier ones, pain comes."

Lalitha said slowly, "But society doesn't tell us that. They say, 'retirement means rest.' No one says, 'retirement means spiritual ascent.'"

Shastriji smiled. "That's why you feel hollow. Because you're trying to find meaning in a chapter that has already turned. Your son is building his Grihastha life. You are being called inward now — to build your Vanaprastha path."

The Ashram Within – A Quiet Shift

That night, Lalitha lit the diya in front of the Krishna idol like she always did. But today, she sat a little longer. She wasn't praying *for* Arjun to call. She simply prayed to *feel full again.*

Jagdish opened the Gita — not to find a verse for teaching — but for understanding. For himself.

He whispered, "This is the ashram now, isn't it?"

Lalitha nodded, "Our own home... is our forest."

Vanaprastha in Action – Letting Go, Leaning In

Over the next few weeks, small changes began:

- They stopped checking the phone obsessively for messages.
- They began visiting the local temple together every morning, walking slowly, hand in hand.
- Jagdish started writing reflections — not about Arjun, but about life, purpose, and what lies beyond the roles.
- Lalitha began teaching bhajans to two elderly women next door, their laughter echoing like girls in school.

They were not retreating.

They were *re-centering*.

The Forest in the Heart – Embracing the Present Stage

One morning, Jagdish sat under the mango tree with a thermos of tea. Lalitha joined him with two steel glasses.

"No rush today?" she asked playfully.

"No rush ever again," he smiled.

They looked at the swing once again — still still — but no longer sad.

Shastriji's words returned to them:

"The Grihastha trains you to give. But Vanaprastha trains you to surrender."

They had not been forgotten.

They had been promoted — from caretakers of a child… to seekers of the soul.

Reflection & Realization for Parents:

Problem Experienced:

Emptiness and lack of direction when children no longer "need" them actively — leading to confusion, sadness, and a feeling of purposelessness.

Gita Insight:

The four Ashramas (Brahmacharya, Grihastha, Vanaprastha, Sannyasa) are spiritual stages of evolution. Pain comes when we try to stretch one stage forever. Peace comes when we gracefully step into the next.

Lesson for Parents:

You are not meant to control your child's adulthood. You are meant to master your own evolution. Vanaprastha is not isolation — it is preparation. For deeper fulfillment, for divine connection, for inner stability.

Practical Steps:

- Create a daily spiritual rhythm — even just 15 minutes of silence or prayer
- Reflect on what you are *becoming*, not what you're losing
- Reconnect with spiritual texts or teachers
- Engage in quiet service — listen, mentor, share without needing recognition
- Let your children go lovingly — they are on their own Ashrama path

Closing Thought:

"When the world stops needing you, God starts calling you."

The train of life moves forward — not away from joy, but toward inner freedom. Vanaprastha is not an end — it is your spiritual springtime. Step into it with courage.

Five

The Noisy Compartments – Understanding the Inner Forces

Based on the Principle of the Three Gunas: Tamas, Rajas, and Sattva

"The Inner Train Riot" – Jagdish & Lalitha Witness Their Mind's Passengers

The Loud Neighbor – An Unexpected Disturbance

The shrill voice of the neighbor's television pierced the peaceful evening. Loud news anchors debated angrily while devotional songs from another flat clashed in the background. Lalitha winced as she closed the window.

"This compartment is getting too noisy," she muttered.

Jagdish chuckled, "Not just this one. Ours too."

She looked at him curiously.

He tapped his chest gently. "This compartment inside — full of noise. Worry, blame, regret, hope, memory… they're all shouting at once."

Shastriji's Analogy – The Three Compartments Within

That weekend, they walked with Shastriji to the temple. On the way back, they paused near the railway track to rest.

Shastriji pointed to a goods train passing slowly. "Each of us carries three types of compartments inside — Tamas, Rajas, and Sattva."

Jagdish nodded, "Yes, from the Gita — inertia, activity, and harmony."

Shastriji continued, "When we are stuck in sorrow, laziness, or regret — that's **Tamas**. When we are restless, comparing, craving — that's **Rajas**. And when we feel peaceful, content, and aligned — that's **Sattva**."

Lalitha asked, "So when I cry for Arjun and feel abandoned — is that Rajas?"

"Yes," Shastriji replied. "Because it's desire for how things *should be* — not how they are."

Lalitha's Honest Confession – "I keep checking my phone"

That night, Lalitha finally spoke what she'd been hiding.

"Even when I'm praying, I keep glancing at my phone. Hoping Arjun will call."

Jagdish gently held her hand.

"I still sometimes feel angry when I see others surrounded by their grandchildren."

They sat in silence, facing their own noisy compartments.

Lalitha whispered, "It's like I want to be calm… but my mind won't let me."

Jagdish said, "That's the pull of Rajas. Activity without peace. Longing without presence."

The Gita Reading – A Verse That Lands

The next morning, Jagdish opened the Bhagavad Gita and read aloud from Chapter 14:

"Tamas binds through ignorance and delusion.
Rajas binds through desire and attachment.
But Sattva… illuminates and liberates."

They sat with those words, slowly.

Shastriji, who had just walked in with prasad, smiled.

"You can't destroy Rajas or Tamas by force. You *transcend* them by feeding **Sattva**. Think of it like changing coaches. If one compartment is noisy, you shift. Not by fighting — but by choosing peace."

The Shift to Sattva – Small, Quiet Changes

In the days that followed, Jagdish and Lalitha gently began shifting compartments.

- Lalitha began keeping her phone in another room while praying.
- Jagdish spent 15 minutes daily in silence, watching the flame of a lamp.
- They read one verse together every evening — no debates, just reflection.
- Lalitha made kheer one morning and gave it to the temple — her face glowing.

These were not big acts. But the noise within slowly began to hush.

The Quiet Coach – Living from Sattva

One afternoon, the power went off. No fan. No fridge hum. No TV noise from the neighbor.

Just silence.

Lalitha sat near the window, humming a bhajan. Jagdish joined in softly. Their voices blended like old friends — steady, calm.

They weren't waiting for Arjun. They weren't escaping sorrow.

They were simply… present.

Shastriji's voice from earlier echoed in their minds:

"When you live in **Sattva**, the world outside may remain noisy — but the compartment within becomes your sanctuary."

Reflection & Realization for Parents:

Problem Experienced:

Restlessness, emotional disturbance, comparison, and longing for how things *should* be — leading to anxiety and sadness.

Gita Insight (Chapter 14):

The three Gunas govern our inner world.

- **Tamas** (inertia) binds through ignorance and helplessness.

- **Rajas** (activity) binds through desire, expectation, and comparison.
- **Sattva** (harmony) frees through peace, clarity, and spiritual rhythm.

Lesson for Parents:

Your suffering is not because of your child's actions — it is due to the **Guna** dominating your mind in that moment.

By consciously shifting from Rajas to Sattva — through prayer, study, self-care, and service — you reclaim your peace.

Practical Steps:

- Begin each day with 5 10 minutes of silence before checking your phone
- Light a lamp, offer gratitude, and read one Gita verse daily
- Engage in service — however small — without expectation
- Be aware of your thoughts: "Is this Tamas, Rajas, or Sattva?" and choose accordingly
- Make time for music, nature, or journaling — food for Sattva

Closing Thought:

"When the compartments of the mind become noisy, don't argue with them. Just rise... and shift to the quiet coach."

The Bhagavad Gita doesn't ask you to suppress your emotions — it teaches you how to rise above them. One Guna at a time.

Choose Sattva. Choose stillness. Choose your inner sanctuary.

Six

The Driver's Cabin – Who's Holding the Wheel?

Based on the Principle of Buddhi vs. Manas (Intellect vs. Mind)

"Let the intellect take the wheel, not the passenger of emotion."

The Sharp Turn

The auto jolted slightly as it turned near the curve of the old Mandir lane. Jagdish, who rarely reacted, suddenly held tighter to the handle. Lalitha looked up from her cloth bag filled with vegetables.

"Everything okay?" she asked softly.

Jagdish nodded but his eyes stayed fixed on the road. The auto driver seemed distracted — weaving through traffic without focus, humming loudly, and often glancing at his phone.

Shastriji, who was seated beside them, calmly observed the driver's antics and said gently,

"Life is like this auto ride. If the driver — the intellect — is alert, the journey is safe. But if the mind starts grabbing the wheel, we sway in all directions."

The Inner Collision

Back home, Jagdish sat with his tea untouched. The scene from the road had stirred something deeper.

Lalitha spoke gently, "You were lost in thought even before we sat in the auto. Was it Arjun's call again?"

He didn't respond. The truth was — Arjun hadn't called in over three weeks. The last time, the conversation ended with Jagdish saying, *"You didn't even ask about Ma's check-up."* To which Arjun had replied lightly, *"Oh sorry, I forgot. Got caught up."*

Jagdish's mind had been replaying that scene on loop:

"He should have cared more."
"We raised him better."
"How can he forget something so basic?"

Shastriji's Quiet Observation

Later that evening, Shastriji joined them for a quiet walk near the Neem tree in their yard. Jagdish shared his troubled thoughts — not with blame, but weariness.

Shastriji listened without judgment. Then he gently asked,

"Jagdishji, is it your son's voice that's troubling you… or your own mind's repeated echo of it?"

Jagdish paused. The distinction startled him.

Shastriji continued, "The Manas — our emotional mind — keeps looping expectations, memories, and stories. But the Buddhi — our higher intellect — is capable of seeing clearly. Like a good driver, it can say, 'Enough now. Let's take the right turn.'"

When Emotion Becomes the Driver

That night, Lalitha quietly wept while folding Arjun's old school uniform she found in a trunk. She too had been consumed with a silent hurt — *"At least he could send a message to check on us."*

She realized how both she and Jagdish had been passengers in a vehicle steered by pain, nostalgia, and subtle expectations.

A Manual for Driving – The Gita

The next morning, Jagdish sat in the verandah with his Gita. He softly read to Lalitha:

"manaḥ praśāntasya paramātmā samāhitaḥ – when the mind is calm, the Supreme is revealed." (BG 6.7)

He looked at her and said, "Maybe our peace doesn't depend on Arjun's actions... but on how we train our mind."

Lalitha smiled through moist eyes, "Then let's train it together — like we used to train him with bedtime stories. This time, we'll train the mind with Gita stories."

Realigning the Driver's Seat

They started a gentle practice. Each morning, they would sit in silence for 10 minutes. Jagdish would read one verse from the Gita, and Lalitha would reflect aloud on what it meant for her feelings.

Slowly, the loops of thought started fading. Not completely — but enough to know who the real driver was now.

Reflection for Parents: Who's Driving You?

Emotional Trap: *"They should have called, remembered, cared more."*

This repetitive loop often stems from the **Manas** — the mind tied to memories, attachments, and emotional scripts.

Gita Wisdom: The **Buddhi** is the charioteer — it can guide the horses of desire and emotion, if properly trained. Krishna tells Arjuna not to be led by feelings of hurt or expectation, but by clarity of purpose.

Insight: If you find yourself replaying past conversations or imagining future ones, pause. Ask, *"Is this my mind speaking... or my trained intellect?"*

What You Can Practice:

- Morning silence for 5-10 minutes before the day begins
- Read or reflect on one Gita verse a day
- Write down a repetitive thought — and then write what your higher self would respond
- Speak your feelings aloud to a trusted one, then listen for your Buddhi's voice beneath them

Closing Thought:

"The Manas remembers wounds; the Buddhi remembers wisdom. The one you allow to drive, shapes your journey."

Seven

The Ticket Checker – Let Go After Doing Your Duty

Based on the Principle of Karma Yoga: Nishkam Karma

"You did your best as a parent. Let go now, and trust that Krishna will guide your children."

The Torn Report Card

One rainy afternoon, Lalitha opened the cupboard to clear out some old files. Among yellowing school notebooks and greeting cards, she found Arjun's torn Class 6 report card. She smiled faintly at the scribbled "needs improvement" remark, then suddenly remembered how she'd stayed up with him that whole week during exams, feeding him halwa, coaxing him to revise math.

She pressed the paper to her chest. "I did everything, Jagdish. Why doesn't it feel like it was enough?"

Jagdish folded his newspaper and replied gently, "It *was* enough. You were his mother, not his sculptor. Krishna is the one shaping him now."

The Unexpected Refund

That evening, Jagdish came home from the bank with a puzzled expression. "Remember that LIC policy we had forgotten about? It matured. A refund just came — small, but unexpected."

Lalitha chuckled. "Funny, how something you do and forget brings back something later."

Jagdish paused. "That's Karma Yoga, isn't it? Doing your duty, then moving on — without clinging to the fruit. And yet… the fruit finds its own way back."

Shastriji's Spoon of Ghee

The next day, Shastriji arrived unannounced with a steel dabba of warm halwa. As they ate, Lalitha confessed, "Sometimes I feel I failed Arjun — because he's so far, so disconnected."

Shastriji listened patiently, then said, "Let me ask you something. When you made halwa for him all those years, did you do it hoping he'd return the favor someday?"

"No," she said, "I did it because I loved him."

"Exactly," said Shastriji, "That's Karma Yoga. Selfless action, without bargaining for a result."

He leaned forward and added, "Lalitha beti, your role as a parent was your yajna — your sacred offering. The Gita says: *'You have a right to your action, not to the outcome of it.'* That means, your job was to give — not to guarantee."

The Cleaned Storeroom

That evening, Lalitha began clearing the storeroom. Bags of unused toys, old board games, Arjun's cricket bat — memories stored like emotional anchors. She dusted everything, sorted what could be donated, and packed the rest with a whisper of gratitude.

Jagdish watched her quietly. "Letting go?"

She smiled. "Not of the memories. Just of the need for them to mean something else."

The Flame That Burns On

That night, they lit the diya together before the Krishna idol. Lalitha whispered, "I always thought parenting was about molding. But maybe it's more about offering."

Jagdish nodded, "You poured love into him. Like ghee into the yajna fire. What he does with it now… is between him and Krishna."

Reflection & Realization for Parents: The Ticket of Karma Yoga

The Struggle: Feeling like love and sacrifice as a parent were wasted if children drift away

Gita Insight: *"Karmanye vadhikaraste, ma phaleshu kadachana"* – You have the right to action, not to its outcomes

Lesson for Parents:

- True parenting is an offering, not an investment
- You were never meant to guarantee results — only to give with love and let go with faith

Practical Shifts:

- If you find yourself thinking, *"I did so much and got nothing back"*, pause and reframe: *"I gave because it was my Dharma."*
- Write a letter (even if never sent) listing all you did for your child — and burn it as a sacred offering
- Focus on daily actions of love, devotion, and service — not on waiting for validation
- Say this Gita mantra silently: *"I offer, I release, I trust."*

Closing Thought:

"The parent's duty ends not in outcome, but in offering. Once your ticket is checked — walk forward. The Divine Conductor will take care of the rest."

Eight

The Route Map – The Soul's Journey

Based on the Principle of Jnana Yoga: Understanding the Self (Atma) vs. the Body (Deha)

"The Blurred Family Photo" – Jagdish & Lalitha Reflect on Ownership and Identity

The Trunk with Old Photographs

The afternoon sun poured in through the window, slanting over the wooden floor of the ancestral room. Lalitha sat cross-legged beside an open trunk, her fingers gently tracing old photographs—sepia-toned, faded at the edges, worn by time and memory.

"Do you remember this one?" she held up a picture of their son, barely five, trying to balance a bicycle with training wheels. Jagdish looked over her shoulder and smiled faintly. "He was so stubborn. Refused to let me hold the seat."

Lalitha sighed. "And now… I feel I don't even know what he's thinking anymore."

There was no bitterness in her voice, only a quiet ache.

Jagdish sat beside her, watching the layers of dust dance in the light. "Strange, isn't it? We raise them, feed them, pour our entire lives into them—and yet, they don't belong to us."

Lalitha paused. "What do you mean, they don't belong to us?"

A Sacred Verse, A Sudden Shift

He reached for the Gita resting on the windowsill. "Chapter Two," he said softly, flipping the pages. "Just listen."

'Dehino'smin yathā dehe kaumāraṁ yauvanaṁ jarā
tathā dehāntara-prāptir dhīras tatra na muhyati'

"As the embodied soul continuously passes from childhood to youth to old age, the soul similarly passes into another body at death. The wise are not deluded by this."

Lalitha leaned back, her eyes resting on the neem tree outside. "So, we're only caretakers of these bodies?"

He nodded. "Exactly. Even of our children. They are not 'ours' in the possessive sense. They are souls—eternal, timeless, on their own journeys."

The Blurred Photo

She picked up another photo, this one torn at the corner— a family portrait from years ago. Their children stood beside them, all smiles. But now, the ink had smudged slightly over their faces.

Lalitha whispered, "This photo used to feel like home. Now it just feels... blurry."

Jagdish looked at her gently. "Because the identities in it were never fixed. They're all shifting roles—mother, father, daughter, son. But behind those roles, we're all souls. Temporary travelers on the same train."

The Guilt That Lingers

"I still feel like I failed as a mother," Lalitha admitted, her voice breaking. "Maybe I didn't guide them right. Maybe if I had done things differently..."

Jagdish took her hand. "You fulfilled your dharma. But the results are not in your control. That's karma yoga. And this—" he tapped the Gita—"is Jnana Yoga. Knowing that your children's paths are shaped by their own karma, not your guilt."

From Possession to Compassion

She closed her eyes. "So the pain I feel—it's because I believed they were mine to mold, to fix, to hold forever."

He smiled. "Yes. It's not about detachment of love. It's about detachment from ownership. Real love lets go, not with rejection, but with reverence—for the soul that must walk its own path."

A New Map in the Mind

As dusk fell, Lalitha rolled up the old photos and placed them back with care. This time, not with sadness—but with surrender.

She whispered softly, "I will still love them... but now I will love their souls, not just their forms."

Jagdish nodded, eyes moist but peaceful. "That's Jnana Yoga, Lalitha. The true route map. Not from here to there, but from illusion to truth."

Reflection & Realization for Parents: The Route Map of Jnana Yoga

The Struggle: Parents often see their children as extensions of themselves. When children drift or change, it feels like betrayal or failure.

Gita Insight: "As the embodied soul passes through childhood, youth, and old age, so also it passes into another body..." – *Bhagavad Gita 2.13*

Lesson for Parents:

- You do not own your children; you accompany their soul's journey
- Attachment to roles blinds us to the eternal soul beneath
- You are not the potter. You are the witness and guide

Practical Shifts:

- Replace "my son/daughter" with "a soul I was blessed to raise"

- Each time a painful memory arises, say: "I honor the soul's path, not my plan."
- Gently burn or archive old mementos with a prayer: "May their journey be guided by the Divine."
- Read or reflect on *Bhagavad Gita 5.18*: "The wise see all beings with equal vision—whether a brahmana, a cow, an elephant, a dog…"

Closing Thought:

"You do not own the travelers. You just walk with them until their next station arrives. Let the soul in you bow to the soul in them."

Nine

The Emergency Brake – Holding Still When Life Shakes

Based on the Quality of Sthitaprajna (Steady Wisdom)

"When Brakes Jolt, Stillness Saves" – Jagdish & Lalitha Confront Sudden Pain

The Phone Call That Froze Everything

It was just after lunch. The ceiling fan whirred lazily above the dining table where Jagdish was peeling an orange. Lalitha was folding clothes when the phone rang.

She picked it up — it was Arjun.

But something was off.

"Amma, can you sit down?" he said.

In a few minutes, the stillness of the house deepened.

Arjun's company had shut down. His visa situation was uncertain. There were murmurs about returning to India. His voice carried panic, helplessness, a tone they hadn't heard since he was a child.

Lalitha sat down hard on the edge of the bed. Jagdish, calm on the outside, folded the orange peel methodically.

"Why Us Again?"

Later that evening, Lalitha's voice cracked.

"We finally stopped expecting, stopped hoping… and now this? Why does life keep pulling the brake just when the train feels like it's moving?"

She stared blankly at the wall.

"This feels like punishment," she said. "For loving too much. For letting go too late. Or maybe too soon."

Jagdish looked at her. "It's not punishment," he said softly. "It's a test of balance."

Shastriji's Parable – The Bowl of Oil

Shastriji arrived the next morning. Word had already spread — Jagdish had quietly called him the night before.

Listening carefully, Shastriji smiled sadly. "This is where the Gita becomes not just wisdom — but medicine."

He told a story:

"Krishna once told Arjuna, *'Even a man of steady wisdom is shaken, but he returns to stillness quicker.'"*

Then he brought out an old steel bowl, filled it with oil, and placed a lit diya in it. "Try walking with this," he told Lalitha, "and keep the flame steady."

She took it, trembling slightly. "It's hard," she said, walking slowly, eyes focused on the flame.

"Exactly," Shastriji said. "That's Sthitaprajna. Life will shake — your job is to hold the inner flame steady."

Jagdish's Quiet Resolve

That night, Jagdish didn't react with fear or opinions. He didn't give Arjun advice. He just listened.

"You do what you must, beta," he told him. "We are here — steady. You don't need to carry our worry too."

Lalitha was surprised. "How can you stay so calm?"

He smiled. "I was not always. But now I realize — Krishna is the train driver. We are just passengers. The emergency brake isn't our failure. It's His signal to pause. To observe."

Acceptance — Not Resignation

Over the next few days, the anxiety lessened.

Lalitha, instead of calling Arjun twice a day to check, began chanting in the early mornings again. Jagdish restarted his old practice of copying one Gita shloka by hand each morning, then reflecting on it.

The brakes hadn't been released yet. Arjun's future was still uncertain. But their suffering had stopped.

Because the panic was replaced by **presence**.

The Wisdom of Stillness

Weeks later, Arjun called with good news — a new job offer. Things had stabilized.

But Jagdish and Lalitha didn't react with wild celebration. Just a quiet, grateful smile.

"We were tested," Jagdish said, "and we didn't collapse this time."

Lalitha added, "We learned that steadiness is not detachment — it is devotion without panic."

The emergency brake had jolted them — but it had also trained them.

They had stayed in their seat.

Eyes open.

Hearts steady.

Anchored in Krishna.

Reflection & Realization for Parents:

Problem Experienced:

Life suddenly halting — health scares, job loss of a child, emotional jolts, or financial upheavals that reawaken helplessness.

Gita Insight (Chapter 2.56):

"One who is not disturbed in sorrow, not elated in happiness — such a person is of steady wisdom."

Sthitaprajna is not about having no emotions — it is about not being ruled by them.

Lesson for Parents:

You will feel pain — but you don't have to add suffering to it. Steadiness is not coldness. It's sacred resilience. Your children may panic — but you can be their emotional anchor.

Practical Steps:

- When bad news comes, **pause** before reacting. Don't spiral.
- Create a daily stillness practice — chanting, journaling, walking with breath awareness.

- Remind yourself: *"This too shall pass."*
- Stay connected to **Krishna or your Ishta Devata** — faith makes steadiness easier.
- Let your calm be a gift to your family — not your control.

Closing Thought:

"Pain is a visitor. Suffering is when we give it a room and serve it tea."

Let pain come and go — but remain rooted, as the Gita teaches. Be the emergency brake, not the wreck.

Ten

The Meditation Compartment – Where the Noise Ends

Based on the Principle of Dhyana Yoga: Silence heals.

"Begin a simple meditation practice. Listen to Gita. Chant Krishna's name. It will soften the pain."

A Quiet Morning – The Day Without Demands

It was just past 6 a.m. when Lalitha stepped into the courtyard. The sun hadn't risen yet, but the world had — a bird fluttered on the balcony railing, a milkman passed murmuring into his phone.

She stood by the tulsi plant, her palms pressed lightly together, lips moving in a silent prayer.

Inside, Jagdish sat at the kitchen table, tea growing cold before him. His hearing wasn't sharp anymore, but that morning, it didn't matter. There was no sound worth catching.

The house, once bursting with clocks and calls and instructions to servants and children, had slowed to a soft hum.

For the first time in years, the silence wasn't heavy. It was almost… welcome.

The Inner Noise – And Its Echo

Later that morning, Lalitha folded clothes on the bed — one of Arjun's old t-shirts among them. She paused.

Why didn't he call this week? It's been ten days. Maybe something's wrong? Or maybe... he's tired of us.

Her thoughts raced. Unchecked. Uninvited. She sat down, overwhelmed not by the memory of her son — but by the commentary her mind attached to it.

Jagdish entered, sensing her tension.

"You know," he said slowly, "the real noise isn't outside anymore. It's in here." He tapped his temple. "Thoughts, regrets, stories that play again and again…"

She looked up. "How do we shut them off?"

The Gita in the Ears – An Accidental Beginning

That afternoon, as Jagdish lay resting, Lalitha picked up his phone to play bhajans. But instead, an old recording began:

"When the yogi, by practice, controls the mind... then he finds peace. Gita – Chapter 6."

She let it play. Slowly. Word by word.

She didn't understand every Sanskrit line, but the voice — calm, deliberate — began to wash over her.

For the next 20 minutes, she just listened. Not to find meaning. Not to understand Arjun. Just to… be.

Shastriji's Visit – The Real Meditation

The next day, Shastriji arrived with a thermos of tulsi tea.

"You both look… different today," he smiled.

"We were quiet yesterday," Jagdish replied, "but not in a sad way. In a full way."

Shastriji nodded, "That's the Meditation Compartment."

Lalitha smiled faintly. "Is it that simple? Just sit and listen to the Gita?"

"Yes," he said. "That's where Dhyana Yoga begins — not in Himalayan caves, but in the silence **between reactions**."

"Dhyana," he continued, "isn't the absence of thought. It's the quiet **watching** of thought, until it no longer controls you."

Their New Ritual – Five Minutes of Stillness

That evening, they didn't switch on the news.

Lalitha lit a small diya before the tulsi. Jagdish pulled out the old pocket-sized Gita and read aloud one verse.

They didn't chant loudly. Just once, slowly:

"Hare Krishna Hare Krishna, Krishna Krishna Hare Hare..."

And again. And again.

Not to *achieve* peace. But to make peace *welcome*.

Reflection & Realization for Parents:

Experienced:

Mental exhaustion from overthinking, ruminating, and constantly replaying emotional wounds — especially tied to children's distance or neglect.

Gita Insight (Chapter 6):

"When the mind is conquered, it rests in peace. The yogi delights in the Self."

Meditation isn't about stopping life — it's about stilling the storm inside so the soul can speak.

Lesson for Parents:

You don't need to shout to be heard by the Divine. You don't need to keep thinking to be a good parent. Just *sit. Breathe. Repeat His name.* The silence will start to heal you.

Practical Steps:

- **Five Minutes Daily:** Sit with eyes closed. No phone. No solving. Just breath and name.
- **Play the Gita Audio:** While folding clothes, resting, or walking. Let it absorb in the background.
- **Chant with Mala or Fingers:** One name at a time. Mind will wander — just return.
- **Avoid Stimulation:** Switch off news or gossip calls after 7 p.m. Let the evening be for restoration.
- **Create a Sacred Corner:** A small mat, diya, and picture of Krishna. Let it hold your stillness.

Closing Thought:

"You don't have to fix everything to find peace.

You just have to be quiet enough to feel Krishna's presence within."

Eleven

The Divine Announcements – When Love Finds You First

Based on the Principle of Bhakti Yoga: Tune into God's love.

"Children may forget, but Krishna never does. He is your eternal well-wisher."

The Missed Call – A Familiar Ache

It was a cloudy afternoon. Jagdish reclined in his old chair, the Gita open on his chest. Lalitha stood in the kitchen stirring dal, her eyes often drifting to the phone on the countertop.

A *ping* finally came — but it was an electricity bill reminder. Not Arjun.

Lalitha sighed. "We raised him with such love, Jagdish. How can he forget?"

Jagdish looked up quietly. "Maybe… he didn't forget. Maybe he just… misplaced us. In a corner of his life."

The pain in his voice was honest — not angry. Just weary.

The Temple Loudspeaker – An Unexpected Message

That evening, as dusk settled, the temple loudspeaker began its usual bhajans. But today, the song was different.

"Yashoda ke nandlala, Brij ke rakhwale…"

The familiar tune of Krishna's leelas filled the air, and Lalitha, mid-prayer at the tulsi plant, froze. Her eyes welled up.

She whispered, "How can I miss someone who was never mine to begin with?"

Jagdish joined her in silence.

The God Who Doesn't Forget

The next day, Shastriji came again, carrying two fresh garlands of tulsi.

He noticed the tension in Lalitha's shoulders.

"You look like someone waiting for someone else to love you," he said gently.

Lalitha forced a smile, "Aren't we all?"

Shastriji leaned in. "But Krishna never stops loving you. Arjun might forget birthdays, festivals, even your health — but Krishna remembers the day you cried for Him at age ten. He remembers every lamp you lit, every tulsi leaf you offered, every bhajan you hummed while making rotis."

She looked down, trying not to cry.

"He is the only one," Shastriji continued, "who doesn't require you to be useful, young, or needed. He just wants your love. That's Bhakti Yoga."

The Devotional Broadcast – A Shift in Frequency

Later that evening, Jagdish set up a small speaker by the tulsi plant. Instead of news or politics, they now played soft Krishna kirtans at twilight.

No more doomscrolling. No more checking WhatsApp to see if Arjun had "seen" their message.

Just music. Just the Divine.

In between cooking and cleaning, Lalitha would pause and listen. Sometimes, she'd sing along.

Not because it would make Arjun call.

But because **her heart had found a better listener**.

Love Letters to the Divine – A New Ritual

Soon, Lalitha started writing again. Not to Arjun — but to Krishna.

One letter every week. Honest, simple, sometimes angry, sometimes grateful.

"Dear Krishna, today I missed Arjun again. But I also laughed at a silly memory. I felt You smile. Thank You."

She tucked them into an old steel box beneath the altar. Jagdish found her there one morning.

"You're writing to God now?" he asked.

"Yes," she replied, "because He always reads."

He smiled. "Maybe I should start writing too."

Bhakti is the Train That Comes to You

They didn't chase Arjun's attention anymore.

Some days he called, most days he didn't. But now, they had tuned into another frequency — one where love flowed freely.

Not from expectation. But from connection.

One that didn't depend on wi-fi or overseas schedules.

Krishna had become the child who never stopped visiting.

Reflection & Realization for Parents:

Problem Experienced:

Pain of emotional abandonment, unreciprocated love, and the ache of being forgotten by one's own children.

Gita Insight (9.22):

"To those who are devoted to Me, I carry what they lack and preserve what they have."

Bhakti Yoga is the path of loving God simply, intimately, and unconditionally. Unlike human love, divine love is always returned.

Lesson for Parents:

You are not unloved. You are not forgotten. Your love may feel unseen by your child — but it is **seen by the One who created your child**.

Bhakti is not just temple rituals — it's emotional healing through divine friendship.

Practical Steps:

- **Write to God:** A small notebook or diary. Share your heart — don't filter it.
- **Bhakti Over Broadcast:** Replace some screen time with soulful bhajans or kirtan. Let it play softly in your home.
- **Create a Daily Offering:** A flower, a diya, a mantra — one sincere act of love.
- **Visualize Krishna as Your Child:** Invite Him into your conversations, jokes, even complaints.
- **Remember His Promises:** Re-read Gita verses that reassure. Keep them nearby.

Closing Thought:

"When your child forgets to call, Krishna whispers your name.
When your heart aches for love, Bhakti fills it silently.
You are never alone — you are eternally remembered."

Twelve

The Luggage Rack – Letting Go Gracefully

Based on the Principle of Vairagya (Detachment)

"Release the grip, and you'll feel the peace you've been seeking." – Krishna, quietly within

The Cupboard That Wouldn't Close – Too Full to Breathe

One humid afternoon, Lalitha wrestled with the old teakwood cupboard in their bedroom. The door wouldn't shut — sarees, woolen shawls, unopened gifts, and saved packaging from Arjun's childhood kept spilling out.

Frustrated, she muttered, "This cupboard is like my heart. Too full of old things I can't use, can't give away, but can't stop clinging to."

Jagdish looked up from his seat by the window. He had just folded another letter to Arjun — unsent like all the others.

He said quietly, "Maybe it's time we start keeping only what we truly need — inside and out."

Emotional Inventory – What Are We Still Holding?

That evening, Shastriji visited again, carrying tulsi leaves and home-made prasad. He sensed the heaviness even before they spoke.

Lalitha looked down. "Every time Arjun says he'll call and forgets, I feel like someone has dropped a stone in my chest."

Jagdish added, "I don't even know if he'll come this Diwali. And yet, I keep planning menus in my head... just in case."

Shastriji nodded with compassion. "Do you know what the Gita calls this kind of waiting? *Apeksha* — expectation. And it is the root of suffering."

He paused, then said, "Krishna never said 'Don't love your child.' He said, 'Love without clinging.' That is Vairagya — detachment. It is not coldness. It is clarity."

The Luggage Rack – A Metaphor Revisited

Shastriji pointed to the high shelf in their living room — still lined with dusty trophies, Arjun's childhood toys, and gifts he'd given them over the years.

"You see that luggage rack? It was meant to *store*, not to *hold on to forever.* In trains, people only keep what they can carry. But in life, we carry everything — past festivals, unspoken dreams, old hurts, and expectations."

He turned gently to Lalitha, "Beti, do you know why you feel tired? It's not age. It's emotional weight."

The Quiet Fire - Letting Go, One Thought at a Time

That night, Lalitha did something she hadn't done in years. She opened the drawer filled with Arjun's school certificates, his drawings, and old rakhi cards.

She began sorting. Some she kept. Some she folded with a soft whisper, *"Thank you,"* before placing them in a cloth bag.

Meanwhile, Jagdish gathered the stack of unsent letters. Some he reread. Others he tore into pieces — not in anger, but in release.

They lit a small diya in the courtyard and offered the papers to Agni — fire — as a quiet prayer.

"We're not erasing him," Lalitha whispered, "We're erasing the burden of our own expectations."

A New Type of Prayer - Not for Arjun to Change, But for Themselves

The next morning, during their Gita reading, Jagdish paused at a verse from Chapter 2:

"When a person gives up all desires arising from the mind, and is satisfied in the self alone, he is called sthitaprajna — one of steady wisdom." (Gita 2.55)

Lalitha looked at him. "So peace comes not when Arjun calls, but when I stop waiting for it?"

He nodded. "When we expect from people, we get disappointed.

When we expect from Krishna, we get peace — even if nothing else changes."

She smiled. "Then from today, I expect only from Him."

Reflection & Realization for Parents

Problem Experienced:

Overwhelm and heartbreak from unmet expectations of adult children — hoping for phone calls, visits, respect, or emotional connection.

Gita Insight:

The Gita teaches Vairagya — *true detachment is inner freedom, not abandonment.* You love deeply, but without the chain of expectation. When you release that grip, peace returns.

Lesson for Parents:

You're not losing your child by letting go of expectations. You're regaining your Self. Expectation is weight. Release it to God, and you'll breathe again.

Practical Steps:

- Do a "heart audit" — what emotional bags are you still carrying?
- Choose one recurring expectation (like "He should call weekly") and offer it in prayer.
- Turn attention inward: Start a spiritual practice, rekindle an old hobby, or serve someone else in need.
- Replace "Why isn't Arjun…?" with "How can I reconnect with Krishna today?"

Closing Thought:

"When the luggage is light, the journey becomes easier."

Let go not of love — but of the weight that distorts it.

Place your trust, your hope, and your peace not in your child's actions — but in the divine hands of Krishna.

Thirteen

Delays & Detours – When Life Doesn't Go As Planned

Based on the Principle of Resilience and Acceptance (Gita 2.14)

"You were not forgotten. You were redirected." – Krishna, through life's unexpected turns

The Festival That Wasn't – Again

Another Diwali passed.

The diyas flickered beautifully around Jagdish and Lalitha's courtyard, but there were no footsteps, no laughter, no scent of Arjun's favorite ghee-laden sweets being devoured.

Only silence.

"He said he might come this year," Lalitha murmured, folding the same maroon kurta she had bought for him, now back in the cupboard.

Jagdish didn't reply. He stared out at the narrow lane that once rang with Arjun's childhood chatter.

Detour or Desertion? – Wrestling with the Void

Lalitha's voice cracked as she set the puja plate down. "Do you think this is just how it's going to be now? One message. One excuse. And we just wait again?"

Jagdish rubbed his temples. "We made space for him in our calendar… he filled it with something else."

Shastriji arrived just then, carrying saffron ladoos and a gentle smile. He sensed the ache in the air and said, "You know, even trains get delayed. Some take detours. But they still move."

Shastriji's Story – The Track that Disappeared

Shastriji settled in with his usual tulsi tea and continued:

"Once, during monsoon, the train from Haridwar to Rameshwaram had to be rerouted. The main track had collapsed. Passengers grumbled... but the detour showed them towns they'd never planned to visit. Some said it was the most beautiful journey of their lives."

He looked into their eyes. "What if this silence in your life... isn't abandonment? What if it's a divine detour?"

Accepting the Season – Learning to Sit With the Unknown

That evening, Lalitha lit a small lamp and sat before the Gita. She had started reading one verse a day, just like Shastriji suggested. That day, she reached:

"O son of Kunti, the contact of the senses with their objects gives rise to cold and heat, pleasure and pain. They come and go. Bear them patiently." (Gita 2.14)

She read it aloud. Slowly. Then again.

Tears welled up — but they were softer this time. Not bitter. Just... human.

What the Delay Teaches – Loving Without the Timeline

Jagdish watched her quietly. Then he said, "You know... I don't think Arjun means harm. I think he's just caught in his own traffic. His own karma. Maybe we're not the destination he's heading toward right now."

Lalitha responded, "So we wait forever?"

"No," he said gently. "We don't wait. We move too. Just in a different direction."

Turning Inward – The Other Journey Begins

Over the next few weeks, things subtly changed.

Lalitha began helping a neighbor with her newborn granddaughter — holding the child, singing old lullabies she thought she'd forgotten.

Jagdish gave a talk on the Gita at the local library — his first in years. He ended it with this:

"Sometimes, when a train doesn't arrive, you discover the strength to walk."

That night, they didn't speak of Arjun.

They sat in the courtyard, watching stars emerge — one by one — like blessings arriving in their own time.

Reflection & Realization for Parents

Problem Experienced:

Emotional pain when plans don't go as expected — cancelled visits, forgotten occasions, a sense of being left behind.

Gita Insight (2.14):

Life comes in seasons. Pain, pleasure, connection, and silence — all are temporary. Acceptance of this truth builds inner resilience and grace.

Lesson for Parents:

Delays are not denial. Detours are not abandonment. They are divine invitations — to evolve inward, to love without timelines, and to rediscover meaning beyond family roles.

Practical Steps:

- Stop measuring love by calendar events — release the pain of "should have come."
- Begin a personal practice — journaling, chanting, walking in nature.
- Support others who feel forgotten — a widow, a lonely neighbor, or a young mother.

- Build inner strength through spiritual study — even ten minutes of the Gita can change your emotional climate.

Closing Thought:

"Not all delays are disappointments. Some are sacred pauses — meant to awaken a deeper version of you."

Your child may be walking their own winding track — but your train is still moving.

Stay aboard. Trust the route. The divine conductor hasn't forgotten you.

Fourteen

Train Guide – Trusting the Guru & Scripture

Based on the Principle of Guru & Shastra (Gita 4.34)

"When the map confuses you, ask the one who has walked the path." – Krishna, on surrendering to higher wisdom

The Fog on the Tracks – Feeling Spiritually Lost

A week had passed without any message from Arjun. Not even a forwarded meme.

That morning, Lalitha sat cross-legged on the floor, trying to recite a Gita verse Shastriji had marked for her. But the words blurred. Her mind wandered.

"What's the point of all this?" she muttered. "I chant. I pray. But still the pain remains."

Jagdish looked up from his worn-out copy of the Gita. "Maybe we need more than reading. Maybe we need direction."

Enter the Guide – Shastriji's Gentle Correction

That evening, Shastriji walked in with a cloth bag of prasad and a serene smile. Seeing their restless faces, he sat down slowly.

Lalitha blurted out, "We're trying to be spiritual. We chant. We light diyas. But it's not changing the ache. It still feels like we've been left behind."

Shastriji closed his eyes for a moment. "When you're on a train and it stops in the middle of nowhere, what do you do?"

Jagdish replied, "Wait. Trust the driver knows the path."

"Exactly," said Shastriji. "And on this inner journey, Krishna is the Driver. The Gita is your guidebook. And the Guru is the staff on board — reminding you not to panic, even when the lights flicker."

Lost Compass – When the Child Becomes the Guru

"I thought children were meant to care for us when we're old," Lalitha said softly. "Isn't that the natural order?"

Shastriji nodded, then said something unexpected:

"Sometimes we think our children will become our guides. But if they are lost in their journey, how can they show you the way?"

He leaned in closer. "When your child cannot guide you, turn to Krishna. Turn to scripture. And turn to those who live its truth. That is the true Guru. Not one in robes necessarily — but one who brings clarity."

The New Practice – Becoming a Seeker, Not a Beggar

That night, Jagdish opened his Gita again — not as a book of rules, but as a living voice.

He read slowly:

"Approach a Guru with humility, inquiry, and service. They will impart knowledge as they have seen the truth." (Gita 4.34)

For the first time, he didn't read it *for* Arjun, hoping it would change him.

He read it *for* himself. To walk forward, instead of waiting behind.

A Different Light – Inner Parenting

In the following days, something began to shift.

Lalitha began waking up earlier — not to check her phone, but to sit quietly in prayer. She began listening to soft Gita recitations while doing her chores.

Jagdish joined a weekly satsang at the temple with Shastriji, where they reflected on how to live Gita in everyday life — as householders, not just monks.

They stopped parenting the past.

They started parenting their inner growth.

Who Is Really Guiding You?

One morning, Jagdish turned to Lalitha and said, "You know... Arjun gave us life's purpose for decades. But now? It is Krishna who is showing us the way. Arjun was just one chapter. Not the entire book."

Lalitha smiled, her eyes moist but peaceful. "Then maybe this silence… isn't a punishment. It's space for new guidance to enter."

She looked toward the Gita, then at the temple bell ringing faintly in the distance. "We were so busy waiting for someone to return — we didn't notice that Krishna had never left."

Reflection & Realization for Parents

Problem Experienced:

Frustration that despite spiritual effort, peace is elusive; confusion when children are unable or unwilling to offer emotional support or guidance.

Gita Insight (4.34):

True guidance comes from the Guru and Shastra — not from emotional dependence on those still caught in their own journey. A sincere seeker will always find their next teacher.

Lesson for Parents:

You are no longer just givers. You are seekers now. Look up — not around. When children cannot lead you forward, Krishna will. Through the Gita, saints, or even quiet intuition.

Practical Steps:

- Choose one verse of the Gita to reflect on each day — even 5 minutes counts.
- Find a spiritual mentor — a local teacher, a trusted elder, or a satsang group.
- Stop trying to change your children's path — change your relationship to your own.
- Keep asking: *"Who is my guide right now?"* Shift from emotional

hope to spiritual trust.

Closing Thought:

"When your child cannot hold your hand, Krishna will."

Don't let disappointment dim your inner light.

Your journey is not dependent on who walks with you — but on whether you are moving toward truth.

The Train Guide has always been there.

Just waiting for you to ask for directions.

Fifteen

Final Destination – Krishna, the Eternal Home

Based on the Principle of Surrender (Sharanagati & Gita 18.66)

"You are not just parents. You are souls in search of shelter — and Krishna is waiting."

The Platform of Letting Go – A Quiet Evening

The air was cooler that evening. The neem tree's shadow stretched long across the courtyard. Jagdish and Lalitha sat on the swing together — no phone in hand, no expectation in their gaze.

Arjun hadn't called in weeks. There was no promise of a visit.

But for once, the silence didn't ache — it simply *was.*

Lalitha gently said, "Do you think he'll ever come back?"

Jagdish closed his eyes, then replied, "Maybe not in the way we imagined."

He reached into his kurta pocket and pulled out a folded note — a verse he had scribbled from his recent Gita reading:

"Abandon all varieties of dharma and just surrender unto Me. I shall deliver you from all sin. Do not fear." (Gita 18.66)

The Last Message – Shastriji's Visit

A few days later, Shastriji visited one last time before his annual pilgrimage. He looked at the peaceful faces of Jagdish and Lalitha and smiled.

"You've arrived," he said softly.

"Arrived where?" asked Lalitha, confused.

"At the station where longing ends… and love begins," he replied. "You are no longer waiting for your son. You're walking toward your true Home now — Krishna's heart."

He handed Jagdish a tulsi mala and said, "Your train is not ending — it's finally reaching its real destination."

Letting Go of the Last Luggage – The Final Release

That night, Lalitha lit a small diya and placed it before the family altar. She folded her hands and whispered:

"Krishna, I gave birth. I raised. I loved. But now, I return it all to You. The joy. The pain. The memory. The longing. It was never mine."

She turned to Jagdish and asked, "Do you still wish he'd call?"

Jagdish smiled, "I wish him peace — wherever he is. But I don't wait anymore. I walk now. Toward something greater."

The Train Arrives – A Spiritual Return

Weeks turned into months. Arjun's absence remained. But the house transformed.

The once dull veranda now hosted weekly Gita study circles.

Lalitha began composing bhajans, her voice trembling but pure.

Jagdish gave talks on karma and detachment at the temple.

They had not just accepted their son's distance — they had transcended it.

They had boarded the final leg of their journey: the inward train toward Krishna.

A Home That Never Leaves

One dusk, as the sun painted the sky orange, Lalitha whispered, "We were looking for home in the wrong place, weren't we?"

Jagdish nodded. "Yes. Arjun built a home abroad. But Krishna built one in our hearts. And we forgot to live in it."

She placed her head on his shoulder. "I think we're home now."

He looked up at the peepal tree, its leaves shimmering in the breeze, and replied, "Yes. Not the house we built for our children — but the home Krishna built for us. Eternal. Undemanding. Always open."

Reflection & Realization for Parents

Problem Experienced:

Deep pain from emotional abandonment, the ache of never getting closure or return from children who've moved on.

Gita Insight (18.66):

True shelter is not in roles or people — but in surrender to the Divine. Let go of all attachments and fears. Krishna is the final destination, the only One who never leaves.

Lesson for Parents:

You are not homeless just because your children moved on. Your true home has always been with Krishna. When you surrender the pain, the stories, the expectations — peace floods in. That is Moksha.

Practical Steps:

- Say the Gita 18.66 verse daily as a prayer — not to escape, but to return
- Replace questions like "Why did this happen?" with "Where is Krishna in this?"
- Make your spiritual space a living altar — chant, reflect, be still
- Write a letter to Krishna surrendering every expectation that still clings
- Accept: closure doesn't come from others. It comes from surrender.

Closing Thought:

"Your child may forget you. But Krishna remembers every tear."

He was never gone.

He was simply waiting for you to stop looking out the window…

and step off the train into His arms.

The journey is complete.

Not because your child returned.

But because *you did.*

You returned… to your Self.

To peace.

To Krishna.

To Home.

Sixteen

The Unseen Luggage – Why People Suffer

Based on the Principle of Shadripu (The Six Inner Enemies)

"Most pain isn't from what others did. It's from what we carry inside, unknowingly."

Featuring Jagdish & Lalitha's final inner journey.

The Weighing Room – A Quiet Realization

The monsoon clouds had rolled in. The veranda smelled of wet earth. Jagdish sat near the window, watching the rain fall gently on the tulsi pot.

Lalitha was reading a slim spiritual book Shastriji had left behind — the cover simply said: *"The Six Enemies Within."*

She looked up and asked, "Jagdish, what if our sorrow was never really because of Arjun... but because of something in us?"

He turned slowly, eyebrows furrowed, "What do you mean?"

She began reading aloud:

"Shadripu — the six enemies that live in every human heart:

- **Kama** – Unfulfilled desire
- **Krodha** – Anger at unmet expectations
- **Lobha** – Wanting more than what is
- **Moha** – Blind attachment
- **Mada** – Subtle pride
- **Matsarya** – Jealousy of others' joy"

She whispered, "Maybe our pain isn't just from what Arjun forgot... but from what we refused to release."

Shastriji's Final Message – The Inner Enemies

The next morning, Shastriji came by with a small gift — a wooden box labeled *"The Luggage Rack Within."*

He opened it gently to reveal six pebbles — each with one Sanskrit word carved on it: **Kama. Krodha. Lobha. Moha. Mada. Matsarya.**

"These," he said, "are heavier than any baggage your child can leave behind. These are what weigh the soul down."

Lalitha stared at the pebble marked *Moha* (attachment) and said, "So we suffer because of these?"

Shastriji nodded, "Yes. These six hijack the mind. They create false stories:

'My child owes me,'

'I deserve this,'

'Others are better off,'

'Why me?'"

He smiled gently, "It's not your child causing the suffering. It's the expectation that they must behave a certain way. That's **Kama** and **Moha**."

Jagdish held the *Krodha* pebble and whispered, "Then all this resentment… it's our own doing?"

Shastriji replied, "Gita doesn't just teach how to act — it teaches what to drop."

The Mirror Within – Seeing the Real Cause

That night, Jagdish and Lalitha sat beside their home altar.

They didn't pray for Arjun to return.

They didn't cry over the past.

Instead, they placed each pebble on the floor and lit a small diya in front of it.

Then, one by one, they faced each Shadripu — not with guilt, but with grace.

Kama – *Unfulfilled Desire*

Lalitha picked up the first pebble.

"I always dreamed Arjun would live nearby. Call every day. Celebrate every Diwali with us."

Her voice softened, "But I didn't want a son. I wanted *my version* of him. That was **Kama**."

She placed the pebble on the floor.

"I release this longing. Let him be. And let me learn to be — with Krishna."

Krodha – ***Anger at Unmet Expectations***

Jagdish took the second pebble.

"I kept replaying the same scene — how he promised to visit and didn't. And I burned."

He looked down. "But who suffered in that fire? Me."

He gently placed the pebble.

"I release **Krodha**. It never changed him. It only consumed me."

Lobha – ***Wanting More Than What Is***

Lalitha's eyes filled as she held the third pebble.

"I had comfort, a husband who listened, even time to read. But I still wanted *more* — more messages, more love, more proof I mattered."

She sighed, "That wanting… never ended."

She placed it beside the others.

"I let go of **Lobha** — and let myself see what already is."

Moha – ***Blind Attachment***

Jagdish held the Moha pebble tightly.

"I loved Arjun. But I also *clung* to the idea that he was mine — as if his life should orbit ours."

He smiled faintly.

"But he's not mine. He's Krishna's."

He placed the pebble down.

"I release **Moha** — the illusion of ownership."

Mada – *Subtle Pride*

Lalitha nodded slowly.

"I told myself — we were good parents. We deserved better. That 'should'... it was pride."

She placed the pebble near the flame.

"I release **Mada** — it made me bitter. I choose to be humble instead."

Matsarya – *Jealousy of Others' Joy*

Jagdish picked up the last pebble.

"There were days I saw neighbors with their grandchildren... and something inside me turned."

He looked at her. "But their joy is not my loss."

He set it down.

"I release **Matsarya**. What's meant for us, will come. What's not, was never ours."

As the flame flickered, something inside them loosened.

Not bitterness — but freedom.

Not a letting go of love — but a letting go of control.

The Luggage Rack is Empty

The next day, the house felt light.

Not because Arjun had called (he hadn't), but because the emotional clutter had cleared.

Jagdish no longer looked at the phone every hour.

Lalitha no longer opened old photos hoping for a feeling.

They sat quietly with tea — not in sorrow, but in silence.

The luggage rack within had space now.

Space for peace.
Space for surrender.
Space for Krishna.

The Train for Everyone

Lalitha later asked, "Shastriji always said our Gita train has 15 stations. But who is this train really for?"

Jagdish replied, "It's not just for abandoned parents."

He held up the Gita and added,

"It's for anyone who has been hurt,
anyone who's clinging,
anyone who forgot they're a soul — not a role."

She smiled. "So the real train is not going outward... but inward?"

He nodded, "And the six enemies?
They don't board with you unless you invite them."

Reflection & Realization for Parents

Core Problem:

We think we suffer because our children left us.

But we suffer because of inner enemies — expectations, pride, attachments, unfulfilled desires.

Gita Insight (All chapters echo this truth):

"Freedom is not in controlling others.
It is in conquering yourself."

The six enemies (*Shadripu*) block the soul from peace.

Gita teaches how to dissolve them.

Summary Table: *Shadripu for Parents*

Shadripu → How It Shows Up in Parenting → Gita Response

Kama → "My child should call, should visit." → Let go of longing. Love unconditionally.

Krodha → Anger at unmet promises → Respond, don't react. Release resentment.

Lobha → "I deserve more attention, more care." → Appreciate the now. Drop craving.

Moha → "My child is mine." → See them as souls on their own path.

Mada → "We were good parents, we deserve better." → Replace pride with humility.

Matsarya → "Look how happy other families are..." → Rejoice in others' joy. Let go of comparison.

Practical Steps:

- Write down which **Shadripu** you most identify with — and gently work with it
- Meditate on a verse like **Gita 2.47, 3.35, or 18.66** daily
- Speak to **Krishna like a friend** — not to ask, but to release
- Serve someone who suffers silently — a neighbor, a widow, a lonely elder
- Say daily: *"I am not abandoned. I am being emptied of ego, so I can be filled with peace."*

Final Thought for Parents:

"Your children may be physically far,

but your true child is Krishna — always beside you, within you, guiding you.

Just as you loved your children without expectation,

now love Krishna the same way.

Let this phase of life be your most peaceful journey inward."

The platform is behind you.
The stations have been passed.
The luggage has been dropped.
And now, finally, the soul can rest.
Not in someone else's house...
But in **Krishna's lap**.
This was never a story of abandonment.
It was a **journey... of return**.

Why Do People Suffer?

Because of the **six inner enemies** that agitate the mind and disconnect us from peace. But when understood through the Gita's lens, each one becomes a mirror for reflection and a doorway to liberation.

The 6 Shadripus – Expanded for Parents:

1. Kāma (Desire)

What it is:

A longing for things to be a certain way — wanting love, attention, recognition, or obedience from others, especially children.

Gita Insight:

"From desire arises anger..." (BG 2.62)

When unfulfilled, desire leads to frustration. When fulfilled, it breeds attachment.

For Parents:

Your desire to be needed, appreciated, or remembered is valid — but don't let it bind you. You did your duty; now desire only divine connection. Let your heart's longing flow toward Krishna — He never forgets.

2. Krodha (Anger)

What it is:

Resentment that children don't call, visit, or "repay" your sacrifices.

Gita Insight:

"From anger comes delusion; from delusion, confusion of memory..." (BG 2.63)

Anger clouds wisdom and deepens sorrow.

For Parents:

Anger burns you more than the other. Let go of "they should have..." Replace blame with bhakti. Say, "Krishna, I surrender my expectations to You."

3. Lobha (Greed)

What it is:

Clinging to control, wealth, property, or emotional power over children.

Gita Insight:

"Triple are the gates to hell – desire, anger, and greed. One should abandon them." (BG 16.21)

For Parents:

Even emotional greed — wanting constant attention — creates bondage. Give with freedom. Love without agenda. Your greatest wealth now is inner calm, not outer control.

4. Moha (Delusion/Attachment)

What it is:

Forgetting the soul nature of your children, and treating them as your possessions.

Gita Insight:

"This body is not the self. The wise do not grieve for the living or the dead." (BG 2.11)

For Parents:

You are not abandoned — you are being redirected inward. Moha makes you say, "I am alone." Wisdom says, "I am with Krishna always." Let this truth dissolve the fog of emotional illusion.

5. Mada (Pride/Ego)

What it is:

"I was the best parent. How can they ignore me?" A subtle superiority that expects reciprocation.

Gita Insight:

"Humility, non-pretentiousness…" (BG 13.7)

True strength lies in letting go of pride.

For Parents:

Yes, you gave much — but so does the sun, without claiming credit. Be like that. Quiet greatness is more divine than loud suffering.

6. Matsarya (Jealousy/Comparison)

What it is:

Looking at how other children treat their parents and wondering, "Why not mine?"

Gita Insight:

"One who is free from envy, friendly to all beings…" (BG 12.13)

Comparison poisons peace.

For Parents:

Each soul has a unique karmic pattern. Your children are on their path. Your journey is sacred too. Instead of comparison, cultivate compassion — for yourself and for them.

How to Heal the Shadripu Within:

- Reflect on them during quiet time or journaling.

- Use each train station from your 15-point framework as a practice ground.
- Replace "Why is this happening to me?" with "What is this teaching me?"
- Turn suffering into **sadhana** (spiritual practice).

Final Thought to Reassure Parents:

"Your real children are not just those you gave birth to, but the virtues you now give birth to — patience, surrender, devotion. Let these children grow within. And let Krishna, your eternal child and companion, fill your empty arms with divine love."

Seventeen

Glossary

Ashrama Vyavastha – Life unfolds in four stages, each with its own lessons: *Brahmacharya* (learning and discipline), *Grhastha* (family and responsibilities), *Vanaprastha* (slowing down, reflecting), and *Sannyasa* (letting go and turning inward).

Bhakti Yoga – Walking the path of love and devotion, trusting the Divine, and opening your heart fully.

Brahmacharya – The student phase of life, focused on learning, self-discipline, and preparing for what's ahead.

Detachment (Vairagya) – Loving and doing without clinging; finding freedom by letting go of expectations.

Dhyana Yoga – Finding stillness and clarity through meditation, connecting to the quiet strength within.

Grhastha – The householder stage, where we nurture family, fulfill duties, and balance responsibilities with our inner life.

Guru – A guide who shows the way, helping us see clearly and move with wisdom.

Indriyas (Senses) – Our senses and mind are our instruments for experiencing life. Learning to master them brings peace and self-control.

Jnana Yoga – The path of wisdom, learning to see life clearly, reflect deeply, and understand our true self.

Karma Yoga – Doing what needs to be done with sincerity, without worrying about results. True joy comes from the action itself.

Krishna – The Divine guide, a friend, teacher, and source of wisdom, showing how to live with love, purpose, and clarity.

Manas (Mind) – The thinking and feeling part of us. When trained, it becomes a servant of our soul instead of a restless master.

Moksha – The ultimate freedom, inner peace, and liberation from worry, attachment, and fear.

Moha (Attachment/Delusion) – Clinging to people, roles, or outcomes, which clouds judgment and causes suffering.

Purusartha (Goals of Life) – Life is about balance: *Dharma* (doing what's right), *Artha* (earning and managing resources), *Kāma* (enjoying life), and *Moksha* (finding inner freedom).

Rajas – The energy of activity and desire; when unchecked, it brings restlessness and impatience.

Resilience (Titiksha) – Enduring life's ups and downs with patience, faith, and calm.

Sannyasa – Letting go of worldly attachments and turning inward, focusing on what truly matters.

Sattva – The quality of clarity, calm, and goodness; it brings balance and understanding.

Saranagati (Surrender) – Trusting life and the Divine, releasing control, and letting your heart open.

Sthitaprajna – A steady, balanced person who remains calm and wise through success and failure, joy and sorrow.

Swadharma – Your own unique duty, aligned with your nature, gifts, and purpose.

Tamas – Darkness, inertia, or ignorance that clouds judgment and slows growth.

Vairagya – Learning to love without clinging, letting go of what no longer serves.

Varna System – Each person has unique qualities and roles: *Brahmana* (teachers and guides), *Ksatriya* (leaders and protectors), *Vaisya* (providers and creators), and *Sudra* (helpers and supporters).

Vanaprastha – The stage of gently stepping back, reflecting, serving, and preparing for a more inward-focused life.

Eighteen

Conclusion

This journey has shown us that life, even when it feels silent or abandoned, never truly leaves anyone behind. Jagdish and Lalitha remind us that:

- Love is not measured by attention, calls, or visits — it lives in every act, every sacrifice, and every quiet devotion.
- Peace comes from embracing one's own purpose, instead of waiting for children to fulfill roles or expectations.
- Each stage of life offers new opportunities for growth, service, and spiritual awakening.

Parents who feel forgotten can discover that their lives are far from empty. Their value is eternal, measured not by what their children remember, but by the wisdom, love, and presence they continue to offer to the world.

Ultimately, this story is a gentle call to remember yourself, reclaim your dharma, and walk forward in love, purpose, and inner freedom.

Epilogue

The Journey of Life Remembered

The house was quiet, but not lifeless. Jagdish and Lalitha sat together, hearts lighter than when this journey began. They had walked through grief, longing, and disappointment, but they had also discovered:

- Detachment does not mean absence of love.
- Letting go of expectations opens the door to inner freedom.
- True purpose is not given by others; it is remembered within.

Through acts of service, creative expression, and self-reflection, they had reclaimed their own dharma. Their days now held meaning beyond waiting — meaning born of love, wisdom, and presence.

The courtyard was still. The old swing stood silent under the neem tree, but in that stillness, life hummed quietly. Jagdish and Lalitha had boarded a new train — not one of longing or resentment, but of acceptance, love, and inner awakening. Each day became a station, each moment a companion, each memory a teacher.

The Stations of Life Remembered

1. **Acceptance** – I honor what has been, without clinging.
2. **Swadharma** – My purpose is unique; I need not live another's journey.
3. **Patience** – Waiting is not loss; it is preparation.
4. **Self-Love** – Caring for myself is not selfish; it is sacred.
5. **Service** – Joy blooms when I give, freely and quietly.
6. **Detachment** – Letting go does not mean letting vanish.
7. **Reflection** – Every tear, every thought, is a mirror for growth.
8. **Gratitude** – Even in absence, there is always abundance.
9. **Wisdom** – Life teaches, even when children forget.
10. **Inner Freedom** – Peace arises when I stop controlling and start witnessing.
11. **Faith** – Trust that love, effort, and intention are never wasted.
12. **Connection** – I am part of a larger, unseen design.
13. **Forgiveness** – For them, for myself, for the paths we cannot alter.
14. **Presence** – The gift of being here and now.
15. **Surrender** – Life's conductor guides, I flow.
16. **Love Eternal** – The bond between parent and child, and parent and self, is timeless.

And then… silence. Not empty, but whole. Jagdish and Lalitha smiled softly, hearts full, no longer waiting, no longer chasing. Their love had transformed — from longing to liberation, from expectation to blessing.

Dear reader, this is not just their story. It is yours too. You, who have loved and waited, who have given endlessly, who have felt unseen — your journey matters. Each day is a station. Each moment, a ticket to presence. And perhaps, just perhaps, this story is the gentle conductor, whispering:

"Pause. Reflect. Release.
And remember — you were never truly alone on this ride."

May your journey be sacred.

May your heart be full.

And may you always know that when children forget, life still remembers — and so do you.

Hari Om Tat Sat.

Afterword

Dear Reader,

This story was born from quiet observation, deep reflection, and love for every parent who has given their all and yet feels unseen or forgotten. Jagdish and Lalitha are not just characters — they are reflections of countless parents whose lives continue to ripple with love long after their children have moved on.

Writing this book allowed me to witness a simple truth: life remembers, even when children do not. Your efforts, your care, and your love are never wasted. Even in silence and absence, the seeds you have sown continue to grow — sometimes in ways you may never see, but always in ways that matter.

If this book stirs your heart, let it be a reminder to pause and honor your own journey. Reclaim your Swadharma, embrace patience, cultivate love for yourself, and allow life to guide you gently forward. The stations of your life are not only about waiting — they are about presence, reflection, and the quiet joy of being fully alive.

May this story inspire you to see the sacred in the ordinary, to honor the love that flows through you, and to remember that your life — your heart — matters profoundly.

With love, reverence, and hope,
Vijayshree R

About the Author

About the Author

Vijayshree Ratanparkhe's journey with spirituality began in childhood, nurtured by a quiet sense of connection with the divine. Over the years, her exploration of the Bhagavad Gita became more than study—it became a compass for life, guiding her through challenges, doubts, and moments of longing with clarity and calm.

Through the Gita, Vijayshree discovered that true strength and love are found within, not only in the world around us. This personal transformation inspired her to share its wisdom in ways that touch everyday life—especially the silent struggles of parents whose children drift away or grow distant.

Her writing gently reminds parents that life's meaning doesn't end with their children's choices. There is a Dharma to rediscover, resilience to cultivate, and a deeper, quieter joy waiting in every stage of life.

Some of her favorite verses from the Bhagavad Gita continue to guide her:

"Do your duty without attachment to its fruits." (2.47)

"The one who has control over the mind is tranquil in heat and cold, in pleasure and pain, and in honor and disgrace." (2.56)

"The one who sees Me everywhere and sees everything in Me, is never lost to Me, nor am I ever lost to him." (6.30)

Through these teachings, Vijayshree hopes to inspire parents to find healing, hope, and purpose—reminding them that life still remembers them, even when children forget.

You can connect with me on:

- https://shreesessencia.com
- https://x.com/Vijayshreerp
- https://www.facebook.com/shreesessencia
- https://www.linkedin.com/in/vijayshree-r-48024aa6

9 789334 417708

Printed at Repro India Ltd.